D1492066

NEWHAM LIBRARIES

90800000137229

Everyone Can cook

Published in 2013 by

OM

Om Books International

Corporate & Editorial Office
A 12, Sector 64, Noida 201 301
Uttar Pradesh, India
Phone: +91 120 477 4100
Email: editorial@ombooks.com
Website: ombooksinternational.com

Sales Office
4379/4B, Prakash House, Ansari Road
Darya Ganj, New Delhi 110 002, India
Phone: +91 11 2326 3363, 2326 5303
Fax: +91 11 2327 8091
Email: sales@ombooks.com
Website: www.ombooks.com

Sponsored by Hindustan Tin Works Ltd
Website: www.hindustantin.biz

Recipe Concepts: Vikas Khanna
Cover Image, Food Styling & Photography: Michael Swamy
Research & Styling: Mugdha Savkar & Ganesh Shedge
Design: Shraboni Roy

Introduction copyright © Hindustan Tin Works Ltd

Copyright © Vikas Khanna 2013

ALL RIGHTS RESERVED. No part of this book
may be reproduced or transmitted in any form by
any means, electronic or mechanical, including
photocopying and recording, or by any information
storage and retrieval system, except as may be expressly
permitted in writing by the publisher.

ISBN: 978-93-82607-32-8

Printed in India

10 9 8 7 6 5 4 3 2 1

Everyone Can cook

Vikas Khanna

Om Books International

Contents

Introduction

Food preservation has been practised as an activity by people almost ever since cooking has been in practise as an organised skill. However, if we see the journey of preservation and its evolution over time, it will come as no surprise that today, the canned food industry rules the food preservation chain like no other. Not only has canned food become an integral part of modern lifestyle, it has also created an environmental revolution.

In very early times, preservation was limited to smoking, salting and curing – methods applied mainly to meats. Drying was the only preservation method used for fruits and vegetables. However, there were no methods to preserve cooked food and food that could be carried on long journeys. When world history started changing, food history changed with it. It is rightly said, "You can't win a war on an empty stomach." When large armies were at work, conquering lands and expanding kingdoms, the only thing that kept them going was food. And large quantities of food that could be cooked quickly and preserved for long became the need of the day. In the 19th century, Peter Durand started a culinary revolution of sorts by successfully preserving food in an airtight wrought-iron tin. This was the beginning of canning as a mode of food preservation, marking the birth of one of the largest and most successful industries in the world.

Since that day in 1810, when Durand created the first version of canned food, others have moved forward inspired by him and his vision of preserving food in a safe and sustainable way, to keep it fit for consumption for years. The can, as we know it, has also come a long way from the wrought-iron tin to the lightweight and high-performance modern steel cans of today. Not to mention the transformation in the range and variety of canned food available in the market. From simple canned soups, meats and broths, the range today boasts of vegetables, fruits, desserts and even complete mini ready-to-eat meals in a can! Canned food today has become almost indispensable to modern kitchens owing to its convenience, easy storage and freshness while preserving high-nutrition value and the promise of a tasty meal which gets ready in no time.

Consuming canned food on a daily basis is not a widely followed practise in some parts of the world owing to several myths regarding the canning process. However, for the record, some facts about the canning process need to be brought to light:

FRUITS and vegetables, once harvested, selected and cleaned are cooked at high temperatures, close to the harvest source, and sealed in airtight cans. Only the highest grade produce is used for canning. Most canneries are located very close to the fields, thus ensuring that the food to be canned is at its freshness peak.

THE entire process is streamlined and takes between 4 to 16 hours from harvest to canning, thus keeping impurities away and nutrients intact.

ALMOST all canned fruits and vegetables are fat free and can be included in a basic balanced diet.

THE food being sealed and preserved in airtight containers, stays safe for consumption for months.

Canning contributes greatly not only in preventing food wastage but also helps protect the environment due to the fact that cans are easily recycled. Steel, the primary material used to make cans, can be recycled infinite number of times without any degradation in quality. Metal – both aluminium and steel – are truly permanent and amongst the most abundant materials available in the earth's crust.

Recycling metal cans significantly reduces energy consumption and high levels of carbon dioxide emissions to the environment. As a means of livelihood too, the canning industry has provided jobs to thousands of families – from farmers who provide the produce to be canned, to people working in the can-making factories and the canneries, those who transport this food to the markets and also makes a significant contribution to the life of rag-pickers who work in the recycling industry. Hence, anyone picking up a can, should be aware of the positive contribution they are making to thousands of families and to the environment at large.

Hindustan Tin Works Ltd (HTW), one of the leading Indian can manufacturer, has taken up challenge to educate consumers about the benefits of canned food and has brought together Michelin-Starred Chef Vikas Khanna, a global leading icon of the food and culinary industry and Om Books International, a leading Indian publishing house, for one of our most prestigious projects, *Everyone Can Cook,* which will help consumers to understand the benefits of canned food while enjoying delicious fresh and nutritious recipes made from canned products.

At HTW, constant efforts are made to promote sustainability of metal cans and in 2010, on the 200th birth year of a metal can we launched the global Canvironment Week initiative to promote the sustainability of the humble can while having a strong philanthrophic base to work with the rag picking commuity.

In India, rag-pickers are considered the main cog in the recycling wheel; they work in underprivileged conditions. For every copy sold of *Every Can Cook,* Hindustan Tin Works Ltd pledges to contribute INR 50 (USD 1) for the upliftment of this underprivileged community.

Sanjay Bhatia
Managing Director
Hindustan Tin Works Ltd.

Everyone Can Cook

Everyone Can Cook! That has always been my philosophy, and through this book, I hope to prove it.

My first memory of canned food goes back to my first Christmas in America in 2000, when I truly found a sense of security at a facility that took me in, in a strange land. This was the kitchen of New York Rescue Mission; I still fondly call it my first home in America. Ever since, I have returned several times to the facility to cook for others who need the same reassurance and comfort. It is here that I first saw canned food and the thought that moved me was how cans were touching lives through food. Back then, I hardly knew anything about the working of the canning industry, and only thought of lives being directly touched by the Canned Food Bank that fed the needy. Also everyone at the facility helped and still help cook food. None of them are trained chefs, yet they participate in the process – no matter how – by washing vegetables, chopping meat or even opening cans! And 'Everyone Can Cook' became my philosophy.

Almost twelve years later, I was pleasantly surprised when I was approached to conceptualise recipes for a book using canned ingredients. I recall seen my friends stocking up on canned food to tide over difficult times. So I read up on the industry. Directly or indirectly, it impacts millions of lives – thousands of families who provide fruits, vegetables, meats, etc., to the canneries, people who work at those canneries, people who transport the cans to the market, those who purchase those cans – even those who collect used cans and take them to recycling centres. Artists too create masterpieces using recycled cans. And the humanitarian in me decided to take up the challenge – for the sake of those people whose livelihood depends on this industry, who knowingly or unknowingly contribute to the Canned Food Bank, who

also support conservation of the environment since cans are recyclable, with no toxic emissions, thus holding in check the degradation of precious natural resources.

It has been a fulfilling mission. And yes, now, everyone 'can' cook these recipes using canned ingredients to create wonderful flavours easily. Not only are the recipes filled with flavours, they are just right for those who would like to learn cooking but are scared to start due to the time involved.

Keep a few simple things in mind like draining beans, vegetables and meats and rinsing them before use or draining syrup from fruits before use, heating the food thoroughly when cooking and, transferring the food from half-used cans to other containers and refrigerating to store it properly. The measures, proportions and combinations of ingredients used work brilliantly but I urge you to add your own signature touches to these recipes to create your own culinary masterpieces!

Vikas Khanna

Caribbean Shrimp Salsa with Crackers (Serves 6)

I personally feel that the smaller shrimp are much sweeter in taste and easy to cook. The combination of shrimp with fruits give it a very tropical feel which is always welcome in parties.

Ingredients

500 gm shrimp (shelled & de-veined)

⅓ cup rice vinegar

1 teaspoon red chilli flakes

1 teaspoon green chillies (finely chopped)

1 cup **canned** pineapple (drained & cut into chunks)

1 cup **canned** mango slices (drained & cut into chunks)

½ cup **canned** sundried tomatoes (drained & cut into chunks)

1 medium green apple (peeled & diced)

1 medium onion (finely chopped)

¼ cup fresh cilantro (finely chopped)

Salt to taste

TO SERVE

Crackers

Method

Fill a large saucepan with water and bring to a boil over high flame. Add shrimp and cook for 3 to 4 minutes or till just done Drain away the water and refresh the shrimp with cold water.

Roughly chop the cooked shrimp and combine with vinegar, honey and chilli flakes. Keep aside for 5 minutes.

Mix in the remaining ingredients and toss well.

Serve immediately with crackers.

Papri Chaat with Spicy Tangy Mandarin Dressing (Serves 6)

India's favourite papri chaat – a sweet n savoury crispy street food gets a new avatar! Generally the sourness in papri chaat comes from tamarind but here I've used lemon, pomegranate and mandarin to create a fresh reminiscence of sourness.

Ingredients

FOR THE CHAAT

2 tablespoons vegetable oil

1-inch piece ginger (grated)

1 small **can** chickpeas (drained & rinsed properly)

½ teaspoon ground cumin

1 large onion (finely chopped)

1 large tomato (finely chopped)

1 medium cucumber (peeled & finely chopped)

⅓ cup fresh pomegranate seeds

Salt to taste

FOR THE DRESSING

½ cup **canned** mandarin segments in juice (roughly chopped)

2 tablespoons lemon juice

2 tablespoons honey

1 green chilli (minced)

1 tablespoon fresh mint (finely chopped)

1 tablespoon fresh cilantro (finely chopped)

½ teaspoon chaat masala

TO SERVE

20 pieces canapé shells

Method

For the chaat, heat oil in a large frying pan over medium flame and add ginger. Add chickpeas and ground cumin and toss well. Cook for a minute.

Toss in the onion, cook for a few seconds, then toss in the remaining ingredients and remove from flame.

Combine all the ingredients required for the dressing. Add to the chickpea mixture and toss thoroughly.

Spoon into canapé shells and serve immediately.

Peach & Sundried -Tomato Chicken Tartlets (Serves 6)

These tartlets are an indispensable part of my home entertaining. Quick, easy to make and always a superhit for Superbowls or great Oscar nights. I always semi-cook them in advance and bake them just before serving which gives me more time to spend with my friends.

Ingredients

FOR THE PASTRY

1 cup all-purpose flour (plus extra for dusting)

½ cup butter (chilled & cut into cubes)

1 egg (lightly beaten)

FOR THE FILLING

4 cloves garlic

2-inch piece ginger

1 large green chilli (stemmed)

1 tablespoon olive oil

2 medium onions (finely chopped)

½ teaspoon cayenne pepper

1 small **can** chicken luncheon meat (roughly chopped)

2 pieces **canned** peach halves (syrup drained away & roughly chopped)

6 pieces **canned** sundried tomatoes

½ cup cream

Salt to taste

Black pepper powder to taste

MISCELLANEOUS

6 tartlet moulds

Method

For the pastry, using your fingertips, crumble the flour and butter together till the mixture resembles breadcrumbs.

Lightly but quickly knead in egg to make smooth semi-firm dough. Wrap the dough in clingfilm and refrigerate for 30 minutes.

Meanwhile, for the filling, combine garlic, ginger and green chilli in a mortar pestle and crush to a coarse paste. Keep aside.

Heat olive oil in a frying pan over medium flame and add onion. Sauté till translucent, and mix in cayenne pepper, chicken, peaches and sundried tomatoes. Cook for 2 to 3 minutes.

Mix in ground garlic-ginger paste and cook for one more minute. Stir in cream, salt and pepper and cook till the mixture thickens. Remove from flame and cool to room temperature.

Preheat oven to 150°C.

Remove the dough from the refrigerator and divide into 6 portions. Place each portion on a lightly dusted surface and roll out into a circle of ½-inch thickness. Lightly grease the tartlet moulds, line with the prepared pastry circles and prick all over with a fork.

Fill the lined tartlet moulds with the prepared filling and bake in the preheated oven for 7 to 10 minutes or till the pastry is golden and crisp.

Remove, demould and serve hot.

Salmon Croquettes with Mixed Berry Chutney (Serves 4)

You can make these croquettes with your choice of fish and though that changes the cooking time slightly, the result is always light and refreshing.

Ingredients

FOR THE CHUTNEY

2 tablespoons lime juice

1 cup **canned** mixed berries (drained)

1 small red chilli pepper (minced)

2 tablespoons fresh mint (finely chopped)

1 teaspoon chaat masala

FOR THE CROQUETTES

1 small **can** salmon in freshwater (drained & mashed)

2 medium potatoes (boiled, peeled & mashed)

1-inch ginger (finely grated)

3 cloves garlic (minced)

Salt to taste

Black pepper to taste (freshly ground)

1 medium egg (beaten)

1 cup fresh breadcrumbs

Vegetable oil (for shallow frying) as required

Method

For the chutney, combine all the required ingredients and mash berries lightly with a fork. Cover and keep aside to allow flavours to merge well.

Combine the salmon with mashed potatoes, ginger, garlic, salt and pepper and mix very thoroughly. Divide the mixture into small portions and shape each portion into a small cylinder.

Heat a griddle or frying pan over medium low flame and brush with oil.

Dip the cylinders in the beaten egg and roll in breadcrumbs. Dust off excess breadcrumbs and shallow fry the mini cylinders or croquettes till golden and crisp, turning over and drizzling with $\frac{1}{4}$ teaspoon of oil. Remove and drain on absorbent paper.

Serve hot with the prepared chutney.

NOTE: The chutney can be stored refrigerated for 2 to 3 days.

Vegetarian Spring Rolls (Serves 4 to 6)

The influence of Chinese cuisine on world cuisine at large is phenomenal. The concept of spring rolls, wontons have entered most world cuisines – the fillings differ from place to place but the overall concept remains as seen here.

Ingredients

FOR THE WRAPPER

1 cup all-purpose flour (plus extra for dusting)

A pinch salt

⅓ cup water

1 teaspoon oil

OR

1 package readymade spring roll wrappers

Oil for deep frying

FOR THE FILLING

200 gm tofu (drained & mashed)

1 large carrot (peeled & grated)

1 cluster bok choy (shredded)

¼ cup **canned** water chestnuts (finely chopped)

¼ cup **canned** bamboo shoots (finely chopped)

8 cloves garlic (finely chopped)

1 tablespoon dark soya sauce

½ teaspoon sesame oil

Salt to taste

Black pepper powder to taste

FOR THE DIPPING SAUCE

1 tablespoon light soya sauce

1 tablespoon sesame oil

2 tablespoons chilli sauce

2 tablespoons honey

2 tablespoons spring onion greens (finely chopped)

6 cloves   garlic (finely chopped)

Method

For the wrappers, sift flour into a bowl with salt and mix well. Gradually mix in water till the mixture comes together to make a firm dough. Knead in oil and work the dough lightly for a minute. Cover the bowl with a damp cloth and keep aside to rest for an hour.

For the filling, combine all the required ingredients and mix very well. Keep aside for 5 minutes, then squeeze out the excess moisture.

Whisk together all the ingredients required for the dipping sauce.

Once the dough is rested, knead for 5 to 7 minutes or till smooth and pliable. Divide the dough into 20 equal portions. Lightly dust a rolling board and roll out a portion of the dough into a thin 3"X5" rectangle. Brush the edges with water and spoon the prepared filling in a cylindrical shape on one side of the rectangle. Bring in the sides and roll the pastry around the filling to make a closed cigar shape. Repeat with the remaining dough and filling.

Heat oil in a wok over medium flame. Carefully slide in the spring rolls one at a time and deep fry till golden and crisp. Remove and drain on absorbent paper.

Serve spring rolls hot with dipping sauce.

Cheese Chilli Soup
(Serves 4)

The sweetness of coconut combined with cheese, chillies and black pepper defines what the comfort for the soul is in terms of balance of taste. You can substitute chillies with red pepper flakes based on how much heat you want in the dish.

Ingredients

FOR THE SOUP

3 cups **canned** vegetable purée

2 cups vegetable or chicken stock

1 large onion (puréed)

2 green chillies (minced)

½ cup **canned** unsweetened coconut milk

Salt to taste

Black pepper to taste (freshly ground)

3 tablespoons processed cheese from a **can** (grated)

FOR THE TOPPING

¼ cup processed cheese from a **can** (finely chopped)

2 tablespoons green capsicum (finely chopped)

¼ teaspoon red chilli flakes

1 teaspoon lemon juice (optional)

Method

Combine vegetable purée, stock, onion purée and green chillies in a large saucepan and bring to a boil over medium flame. When the soup begins to boil, reduce the flame to low and stir in coconut milk, salt, pepper and grated cheese and simmer till the cheese melts. Ensure that the soup does not come to a boil again. Combine all the ingredients required for the topping. Ladle the soup into bowls, sprinkle over a spoonful of topping and serve immediately.

Curried
Corn Soup (Serves 4)

Curry powder is a British way of combining Indian spices in one box, and generally a Western concept of adding intense Indian flavours in one spoon. The proportion and combination of spices varies from region to region.

Ingredients

2 teaspoons vegetable oil

1 teaspoon cumin seeds

1 medium onion (finely chopped)

1-inch piece ginger (finely grated)

1 small **can** cream-style corn

1½ **cans** vegetable stock

1 tablespoon curry powder

1 tablespoon fresh celery (finely chopped)

Salt to taste

Black pepper to taste (freshly ground)

4 tablespoons cream

A few sprigs fresh cilantro

Method

Heat oil in a large saucepan and add cumin seeds. When the cumin seeds crackle, add onion with ginger and sauté till translucent.

Stir in corn, vegetable stock with curry powder and bring to a boil. Add celery, salt, pepper and cream and cook for 3 to 4 minutes more.

Ladle into bowls and serve hot, garnished with fresh cilantro sprigs.

Curry Leaf & Lime Rasam (Serves 2 to 3)

A south Indian aperitif, this rasam enhances your appetite by using the sourness of lime instead of the usual tamarind. Curry leaves are a great source of a light fresh citrusy undertone which combines fantastically with lentils and coconut.

Ingredients

1 tablespoon oil

1 large sprig fresh curry leaves

A pinch ground asafoetida

1 teaspoon black mustard seeds

1 large tomato (diced)

½ teaspoon ground turmeric

2 teaspoons rasam spice blend

½ cup **canned** yellow lentils

½ cup **canned** coconut milk

½ teaspoon black pepper (freshly ground)

Salt to taste

1 tablespoon lime juice

Method

Heat oil in a large saucepan over medium flame. When tiny bubbles appear along the base of the pan, add curry leaves, asafoetida and mustard seeds.

When the spices crackle, add tomato and sauté for 2 to 3 minutes.

Stir in 5 cups water, turmeric and rasam spice blend. Cover and bring to a simmer. When the broth is very fragrant, stir in lentils and bring the soup or rasam to a boil, stirring occasionally to mash the lentils slightly. Reduce flame and simmer for 3 to 4 minutes.

Stir in coconut milk, pepper and salt, cook for 2 more minutes and remove from flame.

Stir in lime juice, ladle into bowls and serve hot.

Fish Noodle Soup with Salmon Pâté

(Serves 4)

This soup is inspired by my travels to Singapore during the World Gourmet Summit. It was served at the reception of the event. The counter serving this had the longest line of people waiting. This is my version of that popular dish.

Ingredients

½ teaspoon vegetable oil

3 cloves garlic (finely chopped)

1 medium red onion (finely chopped)

½ cup **canned** chopped tomatoes with basil

5½ cups fish stock

¼ teaspoon paprika

Salt to taste

⅓ pack noodles

1 small **can** salmon pâté

1 small loaf French bread (cut into 1-inch thick slices)

Method

Heat oil in a large saucepan over medium flame. Add garlic and onion and sauté till translucent.

Add chopped tomatoes with basil and sauté for 3 to 4 minutes. Stir in fish stock, paprika and bring soup to a boil. Reduce flame and simmer the soup for 5 to 7 minutes. Remove from flame and cool to room temperature.

Purée and strain the soup and return to the pan. Add salt, bring to a boil, add noodles and cook till the noodles are tender.

Divide the salmon pâté into 4 equal portions. Using two spoons, shape each portion into a quenelle.

Ladle the soup into soup plates and place a slice of French bread in the centre of each soup plate. Spoon a pâté quenelle on each slice of bread and serve immediately.

Spicy Chicken Corn & Bean Soup (Serves 4)

I generally make this soup when I have a busy day and don't get much of a break to eat well. This easy-to-make soup gives me the same nutrition as a square meal.

Ingredients

1 teaspoon olive oil

4 cloves garlic (finely chopped)

1 large onion (finely chopped)

½ cup **canned** tomato passata

½ cup **canned** red kidney beans in chilli sauce

½ cup **canned** corn niblets

6 cups chicken stock

½ teaspoon red chilli flakes

½ cup chicken (boiled & shredded)

1 tablespoon fresh basil (finely chopped)

Salt to taste

Method

Heat olive oil in a large heavy saucepan over medium flame. Add garlic and onion and sauté till translucent.

Add passata and sauté for 5 to 7 minutes. Mix in kidney beans in chilli sauce and corn and sauté for another minute.

Stir in chicken stock and red chilli flakes and bring soup to a boil. When the soup thickens, mix in chicken, basil and salt and cook for one more minute.

Serve hot with bread rolls.

Tomato Soup with Roasted Pine Nuts
(Serves 4)

Lightly roasting the pine nuts gives them a beautiful earthy flavour which takes this soup a few notches higher. You can substitute pine nuts with walnuts, almonds or any other nut of your choice.

Ingredients

2 teaspoons olive oil

1 bay leaf

2 **canned** onions (finely chopped)

6 **canned** plum tomatoes in natural juice (diced)

3½ cups vegetable stock

1 ½ cups whole milk

Salt to taste

Black pepper to taste (freshly ground)

2 tablespoons pine nuts (flaked & lightly roasted)

A few sprigs fresh parsley

Method

In a large saucepan, heat olive oil over medium flame. Add bay leaf and onion and sauté till the onion is translucent.

Mix in diced plum tomatoes with juice and sauté for another 3 to 4 minutes, then stir in stock and bring to a boil. Reduce flame to medium low and simmer soup till it thickens. Remove the soup from the flame and cool slightly.

Remove and discard the bay leaf and purée the soup till smooth and return to the pan. Stir in milk, salt and pepper and reheat the soup gently. DO NOT BOIL.

Ladle into bowls. Top with roasted pine nut flakes and parsley, and serve hot.

Braised Tenderloin of Meat

(Serves 4 to 6)

Though this dish has traditional Indian flavours, it resonates as a perfect combination of global flavours. Many times I add chopped garlic to this dish in large quantities to give it a new flavour.

Ingredients

FOR THE MEAT

2 dried red chillies

¾ tablespoon coriander seeds

½ tablespoon cumin seeds

2 teaspoons brown mustard seeds

1 teaspoon black peppercorns

½ teaspoon turmeric powder

¼ teaspoon cinnamon powder

500 gm tenderloin of any red meat (cut into 2-inch cubes)

Salt to taste

2 tablespoons oil

½ cup **canned** meat broth

FOR THE SAUCE

3-inch piece ginger (roughly chopped)

4 cloves garlic

2 pieces **canned** jalapeños (drained & rinsed well)

¾ cup **canned** unsweetened coconut milk

2 teaspoons oil

1 large onion (finely chopped)

2 cups **canned** meat broth

Salt to taste

Method

Combine red chillies, coriander seeds, cumin seeds, mustard seeds and peppercorns in a small pan and dry roast over medium low flame till spices are very fragrant.

Remove from flame, cool the spices and combine in a grinder with turmeric and cinnamon, and grind to a fine powder.

Combine the powdered spice blend with meat, salt and oil, and keep aside to marinate for 20 minutes.

Preheat oven to 175°C. Line a baking tray with foil and grease the foil lightly.

Place marinated meat on the tray, sprinkle with 2 tablespoons broth, cover with another piece of foil and braise in the preheated oven for 10 minutes. After 10 minutes, remove the top foil, turn the meat pieces over and sprinkle with the remaining broth. Braise again for 30 minutes or till the meat is cooked and the broth has been soaked.

Meanwhile, for the sauce, combine ginger, garlic, jalapeños and coconut milk in a blender and blend till smooth.

Heat oil in a saucepan over medium flame. Add onions and sauté till golden.

Stir in coconut milk mixture with broth and bring to a boil, stirring constantly. Add salt and the braised meat, cook for a minute.

Serve hot with bread or rice.

Lamb Goulash (Serves 4 to 6)

A world-famous Hungarian stew gets a new twist with the addition of ginger that adds a wonderful flavour to this classic. You can also add your favourite seasonal vegetables to make your own signature version of this stew.

Ingredients

600 gm boneless lamb (cut into 3-inch pieces)

¼ cup all-purpose flour

2 tablespoons oil

3 tablespoons butter (melted)

1 large onion (finely chopped)

4 tablespoons celery (minced)

4 cloves garlic (minced)

2 inch piece of ginger (minced)

100 gm fresh parsnips (peeled & diced)

1 cup canned tomato passata

4 cups canned meat broth

2 teaspoons balsamic vinegar

2 medium bay leaves

2 teaspoons paprika

1 large can mixed potatoes, carrots & peas (drained & rinsed well)

Salt to taste

Black pepper powder to taste

A few sprigs fresh parsley (finely chopped)

Method

Dust lamb evenly with flour. To ensure evenness, sprinkle the flour through a sieve and keep turning the lamb pieces. Keep aside for 5 to 7 minutes to allow the lamb to hold the flour.

Heat oil and half the butter in a large saucepan over medium flame and fry the lamb in 2 batches, turning it over regularly till well browned. Remove the browned lamb onto a plate and keep aside.

Heat the remaining butter in the same pan. Add onion, celery, garlic and parsnips and sauté till the onions turn brown and the parsnips are tender.

Mix in passata and cook, stirring regularly till the passata coats the onion parsnip mixture.

Add the lamb and stir in 3 cups of broth, vinegar, bay leaves and paprika. Cover the pan and allow the goulash (stew) to simmer, stirring at regular intervals, till the lamb is cooked. If required, add the remaining broth.

When the lamb is cooked and the stew has thickened slightly, add canned vegetables, salt and pepper and cook for 2 more minutes.

Serve hot, sprinkled with parsley.

Meat in Goan Green Curry
(Serves 4 to 6)

I still remember tasting this sauce for the first time, on a trip to a Goan spice farm. It was so intense and unforgettable, the flavour of the green sauce. When I first served it at my restaurant, people confused it with Thai green curry till they tasted it.

Ingredients

FOR THE CURRY PASTE

½ cup fresh coriander with stems (roughly chopped)

⅓ cup fresh mint leaves (roughly chopped)

2 large **canned** jalapeños (roughly chopped)

1 teaspoon cumin seeds (lightly roasted)

1-inch piece ginger (roughly chopped)

3 large cloves garlic

FOR THE CURRY

1 tablespoon oil

1 large sprig fresh curry leaves

1 large onion (finely chopped)

700 gm lamb or mutton or any other red meat (cut into large chunks)

2 cups **canned** meat broth

¼ cup **canned** chopped plum tomatoes

½ cup **canned** unsweetened coconut milk

Salt to taste

Black pepper powder to taste

Method

For the curry paste, combine all the required ingredients in a blender with ¼ cup water and blend to a smooth paste. Remove into a bowl and keep aside.

For the curry, heat oil in a large pan over medium flame and add curry leaves.

When the curry leaves crackle, add onion and sauté till pale golden. Add ground curry paste and sauté for a few seconds till very fragrant.

Add meat. Cook for 2 minutes, stirring regularly and stir in the broth. Cover and simmer the curry, stirring at regular intervals, till the meat is cooked and the curry thickens slightly. (Some water may be added if required.)

When the lamb is cooked, add chopped tomatoes, coconut milk, salt and pepper and cook for 1 more minute, stirring continuously.

Serve hot with steamed rice.

Pan-roasted Lamb & Turnips in Curry (Serves 4)

Though turnips are a neutral vegetable, they beautifully absorb the intense flavours of the lamb and the sauce. I generally make this dish in large quantities as it can be used in numerous different ways combined with rice or pasta, giving it a new dimension.

Ingredients

500 gm boneless lamb (cut into large cubes)

1 teaspoon red chilli powder

1½ teaspoons coriander powder

1 teaspoon cumin powder

½ teaspoon turmeric powder

1 teaspoon garam masala powder

2 large onions (roughly chopped)

6 cloves garlic

2-inch piece ginger (roughly chopped)

2 medium green chillies

2 tablespoons oil

2 medium bay leaves

¾ cup canned tomato purée

½ cup plain yoghurt

Salt to taste

Black pepper powder to taste

2 cups canned meat broth

3 medium turnips (peeled, rinsed & cut into large cubes)

Method

In a mixing bowl, combine lamb with powdered spices. Mix well and keep aside to marinate for 15 minutes.

Combine onion, garlic, ginger and green chillies in a blender and blend to a smooth paste.

Heat oil in a frying pan over medium flame and add bay leaves.

When the bay leaves crackle, add onion paste and sauté till it turns golden.

Add marinated meat with any moisture that may have accumulated and tomato purée and cook till the mixture is thick and the raw fragrance of spices has disappeared.

Add yoghurt, salt, pepper and broth and cook, stirring continuously till the curry comes to a boil.

When the curry starts boiling, add turnips, reduce the flame and cook till the lamb and turnips are tender.

Serve hot with rice or bread.

Venison Apricot Stew with Potato Straws (Serves 4)

This dish is inspired by the flavours of a classic Parsee dish. Parsees or Zoroastrians are a group of people who came to India from Persia in the 10th century and greatly enriched Indian culture and cuisine. This dish is traditionally made with lamb. Here, I've used venison to give it a new flavour.

Ingredients

2-inch piece ginger (roughly chopped)

6 cloves garlic

4 dried red chillies (soaked in warm water)

2 tablespoons oil

2 teaspoons cumin seeds

2 large onions (finely chopped)

1 teaspoon cayenne pepper

½ teaspoon turmeric powder

1 cup **canned** tomato purée

2 teaspoons jaggery (grated) or brown sugar

2 teaspoons balsamic vinegar

½ cup **canned** meat broth

1 large **can** venison (drained & rinsed well)

½ cup **canned** apricots (drained well)

Salt to taste

200 gm fried potato straws

Method

Combine ginger, garlic and red chillies in a grinder and grind to a smooth paste.

Heat oil in a large pan over medium flame and add cumin seeds. When the cumin seeds crackle, add onions and sauté till golden.

Add the ground paste, cayenne pepper and turmeric powder and cook for 1 to 2 minutes. Stir in tomato purée and jaggery or brown sugar and cook till the jaggery (or brown sugar) dissolves and the sauce thickens.

Stir in balsamic vinegar, meat broth, venison and apricots. Simmer the stew till thick and add salt.

Serve hot sprinkled over liberally with fried potato straws.

Chicken in Mint Ricotta Cheese Curry
(Serves 4 to 5)

The refreshing flavour of mint is a wonderful addition to savoury or sweet dishes. Fresh turmeric is a seasonal ingredient and has a very different character than its dried counterpart.

Ingredients

1 tablespoon oil

1 large **can** chicken chunks (drained & rinsed well)

2 pods green cardamom

1-inch stick cinnamon

1 cup onion purée

2-inch piece ginger (finely grated)

2-inch piece fresh turmeric (finely grated)

1 large green chilli (minced)

2 cups **canned** chicken broth

½ cup cream

20 leaves fresh mint (roughly chopped)

½ cup ricotta

Method

Heat oil in a frying pan over medium flame, add chicken chunks and sauté till lightly coloured. Remove and keep aside.

Add cardamom and cinnamon to the same pan and when the spices crackle, add onion purée, ginger, turmeric and chilli and cook till the mixture thickens.

Stir in the broth and bring the mixture to a boil. Gradually stir in cream and mint and cook for 2 minutes.

Mix in ricotta cheese, salt and chicken, cook for a minute and remove from flame.

Serve hot with rice or bread.

NOTE: Fresh turmeric resembles ginger and is available in Asian stores. In case fresh turmeric isn't available, substitute with ½ teaspoon turmeric powder.

Coconut Curry Mango Chicken (Serves 4 to 5)

The eternal combination of mangoes and coconut goes a long way in this dish. You can substitute the galangal in the curry paste with fresh ginger. The curry paste also proves to be a great marinade for roasting or grilling meats.

Ingredients

FOR THE CURRY PASTE

2 teaspoons coriander seeds

1 teaspoon cumin seeds

1 flake mace

½ teaspoon black peppercorns

2 pods green cardamom

2 large green chillies

2-inch piece galangal

1 sprig lemongrass

1 teaspoon lemon zest

1 tablespoon fresh coriander root (finely chopped)

8 cloves   garlic

FOR THE CURRY

4 pieces chicken breast

5 tablespoons oil

1 large onion (finely chopped)

1 medium red capsicum (diced)

1 medium yellow capsicum (diced)

1 small **can** unsweetened coconut milk

1 small **can** mango slices (drained well)

Salt to taste

MISCELLANEOUS

Toothpicks

Method

For the curry paste, separately roast dry spices till fragrant and combine in a grinder or processor with the remaining required ingredients.

Rub 1 tablespoon curry paste into the chicken and keep aside to marinate for 15 minutes.

Heat 4 tablespoons oil in a large frying pan over medium flame and pan-fry the chicken, turning regularly till tender. When done, remove, cut into slices and keep aside.

Heat the remaining oil in the same pan. Add onion and reserved curry paste and sauté for 2 to 3 minutes.

Add red and yellow capsicum, sauté for a minute and stir in coconut milk. Bring the curry to a boil, stirring continuously.

When the curry comes to a boil, add chicken, mango slices and salt. Cook for a few seconds and remove from flame.

Serve hot with steamed rice.

Pepper Curry Duck

(Serves 4 to 6)

It's almost unbelievable to look at these tiny humble peppercorns and imagine the intense flavour they hold within them. Their robust flavour combined with the sweetish tang of tamarind takes this dish to a whole different level.

Ingredients

6 tablespoons oil

1 teaspoon black mustard seeds

1 large sprig fresh curry leaves

2 teaspoons black peppercorns (roughly crushed)

1 small **can** unsweetened coconut milk

1 cup **canned** duck or chicken broth

1 tablespoon curry powder

1½ tablespoon tamarind pulp

¼ teaspoon sugar

Salt to taste

6 pieces French duck legs

Method

Heat 2 teaspoons oil in a frying pan over medium flame and add mustard seeds, curry leaves and crushed pepper.

When the spices crackle, stir in coconut milk, broth and curry powder and bring the sauce to a boil, stirring continuously.

When the sauce comes to a rapid boil, reduce flame and mix in tamarind pulp and sugar and cook till the sugar dissolves. Mix in very little salt and remove from flame.

Heat the remaining oil in another frying pan and pan fry the duck pieces till just undercooked.

Add the duck pieces to the prepared sauce, return to medium flame and cook till the pieces are done.

Serve hot with rice or bread.

Sweet & Sour Chicken with Bamboo Shoots (Serves 4 to 5)

I love this dish since the day I first had it in Hong Kong during the shoot of MasterChef India. Though bamboo shoots are used extensively in North- East Indian and Asian cuisines, they can be used in stews and soups to lend an amazing texture.

Ingredients

500 gm boneless chicken

200 ml unsweetened orange juice

4 tablespoons vinegar

2 tablespoons dark soya sauce

2 tablespoons chilli sauce

Salt to taste

Black pepper powder to taste

2 teaspoons oil

6 cloves garlic (finely chopped)

1 medium onion (finely chopped)

1 medium carrot (diced)

1 small **can** bamboo shoots (drained & cut into chunks)

1 small **can** pineapple chunks in syrup (drained & syrup reserved)

1 cup chicken stock

1½ tablespoons corn flour

Method

In a large mixing bowl, combine chicken with orange juice, vinegar, soya sauce, chilli sauce, salt and pepper. Mix well and keep aside to marinate for 10 minutes.

Meanwhile, preheat oven to 180°C.

Place the chicken onto a baking tray lined with foil, sprinkle with 3 tablespoonfuls of marinade and roast in the preheated oven for 12 to 15 minutes, basting with marinade if required.

Meanwhile, heat oil in a wok over medium high flame and add garlic. Sauté till the garlic softens, and mix in onion and carrot and sauté till the carrot softens slightly.

Add bamboo shoots and pineapple chunks and sauté for a minute. Stir in the remaining marinade and stock and bring the mixture to a boil.

Combine corn flour with 3 tablespoons water and add to the boiling gravy. When the gravy thickens, add the chicken with 3 tablespoons reserved pineapple syrup. Adjust salt and pepper and remove from flame.

Serve hot with noodles.

Vegetable-stuffed Roast Chicken
(Serves 4)

I've had this recipe at my restaurant, Junoon, as part of the tasting menu. Small Cornish hens prove to be perfect for individual tasting portions. But here, I use a whole chicken which is great for the family to dine together. With vegetables stuffed inside, it becomes a perfect meal.

Ingredients

1 kg whole chicken (cleaned thoroughly)

Salt to taste

Black pepper powder to taste

2 teaspoons oil

2 large bay leaves

1 large onion (finely chopped)

6 large cloves garlic (finely chopped)

1 large **can** mixed vegetables (drained & rinsed well)

1 small **can** button mushrooms (drained, rinsed well & quartered)

1 tablespoon garam masala powder

1 teaspoon cayenne pepper

Method

Marinate chicken with salt and pepper inside out. Keep aside for 30 minutes.

Meanwhile, heat oil in a frying pan over medium flame. Add bay leaves and when they crackle, add onion and garlic and sauté till the onion turns golden.

Toss in mixed vegetables and mushrooms with garam masala powder and cayenne pepper and cook for a minute. Remove from flame and cool to room temperature.

Preheat oven to 200°C. Stuff the marinated chicken with the prepared filling and roast in the preheated oven for 35 to 40 minutes or till tender.

Carve and serve hot with salad.

Crab & Artichoke Sauce with Spaghetti
(Serves 4)

The delicious aroma of garlic sautéed in butter is one of my greatest memories of visiting Italy on a holiday. During this time I got the opportunity to learn so many different types of sauces and pastas and discovered new combinations like the one seen here.

Ingredients

1 teaspoon butter

4 cloves garlic (finely chopped)

1 medium onion (finely chopped)

4 pieces canned artichokes (finely diced)

1 can vegetable stock or broth

½ cup cream

Salt to taste

Black pepper powder to taste

A few sprigs parsley (finely chopped)

1 small can dressed crab meat (roughly chopped)

400 gm spaghetti

1 teaspoon olive oil

Method

Heat butter in a frying pan over medium flame. Add garlic and sauté for 2 minutes. Mix in onion and half the artichoke and sauté till the onion softens.

Stir in half the stock and bring the sauce to a boil. Remove from flame, cool to room temperature and purée the sauce till smooth.

Return the puréed sauce to the pan and place over low flame. Mix in cream, the remaining artichokes, salt, pepper and parsley and bring to a simmer. Add crab, cook for a minute and remove from flame.

Combine the remaining stock with water in a large saucepan and boil spaghetti till just done. Drain when done and toss in olive oil.

Serve the sauce hot with spaghetti.

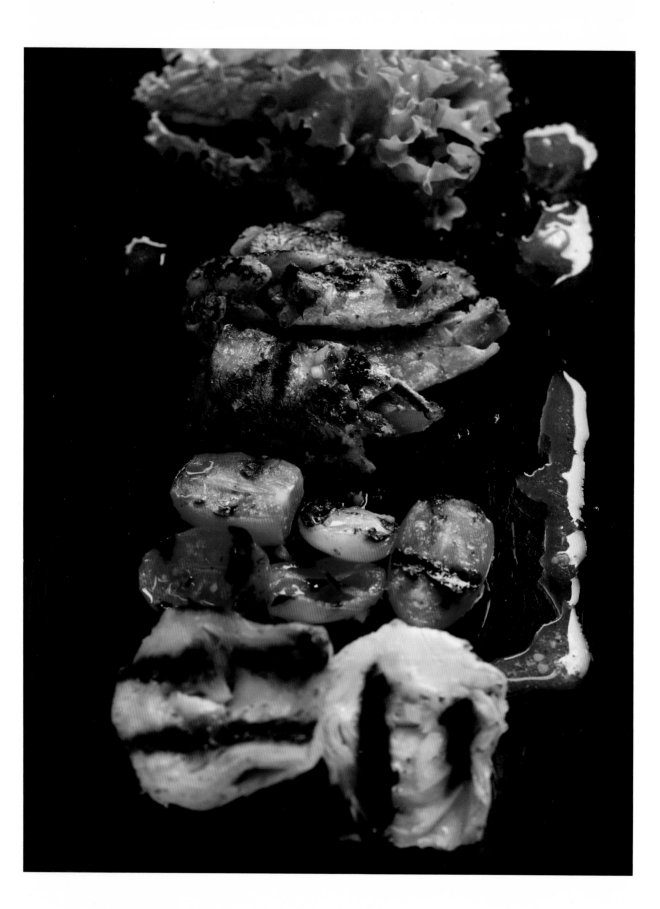

Grilled Sardine & Artichoke Salad
(Serves 2 to 3)

A true definition of a hearty wholesome 'wholicious' meal. It impresses vegetarians and non-vegetarians equally. It's the first dish that hits my grill during my summer barbecues. The honey-ginger combination used in the marinade adds great depth to the flavours.

Ingredients

1 large **can** sardines (drained well)

1 **can** artichoke hearts (drained well & cut into half)

300 gm mixed cherry tomatoes (cut into half lengthwise)

2 tablespoons honey

3 tablespoons mustard

2 tablespoons balsamic vinegar

8 cloves garlic (minced)

2-inch piece ginger (minced)

Salt to taste

2 tablespoons oil

1 head romaine lettuce (torn into pieces)

Method

In a large mixing bowl, combine all the ingredients except lettuce and toss well to mix. Keep aside to marinate for 15 to 20 minutes.

Heat a grill pan over high flame till very hot. Grill the marinated sardines, artichokes and cherry tomatoes for 2 to 3 minutes, turning occasionally, basting with the marinade.

Toss the grilled sardines, artichokes and cherry tomatoes with the remaining marinade and lettuce and serve immediately.

Oyster Soufflé Tart (Serves 4)

I always get company when I make these. The flavour travels to my neighbour's house as soon as these go into the oven. So make sure you always make an extra batch.

Ingredients

FOR THE TART

1 cup all-purpose flour

½ cup butter (chilled)

1 large egg (lightly beaten)

FOR THE SOUFFLÉ

3 tablespoons butter

3 tablespoons all-purpose flour

½ cup oyster liquor

½ cup heavy cream

1 **can** oysters (drained well)

Salt to taste

Black pepper powder to taste

3 eggs (separated)

FOR THE SALAD

1 tablespoon vinegar

½ teaspoon brown sugar

Salt to taste

Black pepper powder to taste

1 small head lettuce (washed & torn)

1 cup **canned** button mushrooms (quartered)

2 medium red capsicums (diced)

1 large onion (diced)

¼ cup **canned** gherkins (sliced)

MISCELLANEOUS

1 large flan mould or
6 individual tart moulds with removable base

Method

For the pastry, using your fingertips, crumble flour and butter together till the mixture resembles breadcrumbs. Lightly but quickly knead in egg to make smooth semi-firm dough. Knead in very little chilled water if required. Wrap the dough in clingfilm and refrigerate for 30 minutes.

Preheat oven to 150°C. Grease tart mould.

Remove the dough from the refrigerator, place on a lightly dusted surface and roll out into a circle of ½-inch thickness. Line the greased mould(s) with the prepared pastry circle and prick all over with a fork.

Bake in the oven for 5 to 7 minutes or till lightly golden. Remove and cool.

For the soufflé, melt butter in a frying pan over medium flame. Add flour and cook till the raw smell disappears. Ensure that the mixture does not change colour.

Whisk oyster liquor and cream together and gradually whisk it into the butter-flour mixture. Mix in oysters, salt and pepper and cook till the mixture thickens slightly.

Remove pan from flame and cool for 2 to 3 minutes. Meanwhile, lightly beat egg yolks and mix into the oyster mixture. Cool the mixture to room temperature. Whisk egg whites till stiff and quickly fold into the oyster mixture.

Preheat oven to 180°C. Pour the soufflé mixture into the prepared tart shell(s) and bake for 30 to 35 minutes.

Meanwhile, for the salad, in a large bowl combine vinegar with brown sugar and stir till the sugar dissolves. Toss in the all other ingredients required for the salad.

Serve the soufflé tart hot with the prepared salad.

Prawns in Tea-infused Coconut Curry (Serves 2 to 3)

To me, this is a timeless creation. It was the first time I used tea in cooking. The excited nervousness I felt when combining tea with prawns was well rewarded in terms of the flavour. Since then I have used tea in numerous sauces and desserts. It's become one of my all-time favourite ingredients.

Ingredients

1 small **can** unsweetened coconut milk

2 teaspoons Darjeeling tea leaves

400 gm prawns (shelled & de-veined)

2 teaspoons honey

1 teaspoon turmeric powder

Salt to taste

1 teaspoon black pepper powder

2 tablespoons oil

1 large onion (finely chopped)

6 cloves garlic (finely chopped)

2 green chillies (slit lengthwise)

1 tablespoon curry powder

½ cup **canned** fish or vegetable stock

4 tablespoons cream

A few sprigs fresh coriander

Method

Combine coconut milk and tea leaves in a saucepan and bring to a simmer over medium flame, stirring continuously. When the mixture simmers, remove the pan from the flame and cool slightly. Strain the coconut milk and keep aside. (Discard the tea leaves.)

Combine prawns with honey, turmeric, salt and pepper and keep aside to marinate for 10 to 15 minutes.

Heat 1½ tablespoons oil in a frying pan over medium flame and pan-fry the prawns with the marinade till the prawns are just cooked. When done, remove from the pan and keep aside.

Heat the remaining oil in the same pan. Add onion, garlic and green chillies and sauté till the onion is translucent.

Gradually stir in the tea-infused coconut milk. Add curry powder and stock and bring the curry to a boil, stirring continuously.

Mix in cream and prawns and cook for 1 more minute.

Serve hot garnished with fresh coriander.

Spaghetti with Mussels in Tomato Coconut Sauce (Serves 4)

East meets West in harmony (not confusion!) here. Just adding a touch of coconut and curry leaves makes this dish totally unforgettable. I often make extra sauce as I like to soak it up with bread.

Ingredients

2 teaspoons oil

1 teaspoon cumin seeds

2 teaspoons coriander seeds

6 black peppercorns

3 cloves

2-inch stick cinnamon

2 dried red chillies

1 small **can** unsweetened coconut milk

1 sprig fresh curry leaves

6 medium tomatoes (finely chopped)

1 **can** mussels (drained well)

Salt to taste

400 gm spaghetti (boiled, drained, refreshed)

Method

Heat 1 teaspoon oil in a small frying pan over low flame. Separately roast spices till they change colour very slightly and are fragrant.

Combine the roasted spices with coconut milk in a blender and blend well till the spices are crushed. Remove into a bowl and keep aside to allow the spices to infuse the coconut milk with flavour.

Heat the remaining oil in a saucepan over medium flame and add curry leaves. When the curry leaves crackle, add tomatoes and sauté till the tomatoes soften.

Remove the pan from the flame and strain the coconut milk into it. Mix well, return the pan to the flame and cook, stirring constantly till the sauce simmers. (Discard the spices.)

Add mussels and salt (if required) and cook for a minute more. Add spaghetti and toss to mix well.

Remove from flame and serve hot.

Chilled Pea Mousse
(Serves 2 to 3)

Long live winters! As a child I used to look forward to winters only for two reasons – one, huddling in a blanket in the cold, sipping hot tea; two, shelling peas warming oneself in the soothing winter sun. During this season the sweetness of vegetables – especially green peas – became the inspiration for this dish.

Ingredients

1 teaspoon oil

1 teaspoon cumin seeds

1-inch piece ginger (finely grated)

2 small green chillies (finely chopped)

1 large **can** green peas (drained & rinsed)

7 to 8 leaves fresh mint

1 cup **canned** unsweetened coconut milk

Salt to taste

1 cup cream

2 sheets gelatine (dissolved)

MISCELLANEOUS
Mousse moulds

Method

Heat oil in a frying pan over medium flame. Add cumin seeds and ginger.

When the cumin seeds crackle, add chillies and green peas and sauté for a minute. Remove from flame and cool to room temperature.

Blend mixture to a smooth purée with mint and coconut milk.

Mix in salt, cream and gelatine. Pour into wet moulds and chill till set.

Serve cold with salad.

Curry Leaf-tossed Baby Carrots & Beetroots (Serves 2 to 3)

When the days start getting shorter and there is a slight nip in the air, two great autumn flavours blossom. The sweet carrot and the earthy beetroot combine in perfect harmony with curry leaves to create a gentle magic.

Ingredients

1 teaspoon oil

1 large sprig fresh curry leaves

2 small green chillies (minced)

3 shallots (finely chopped)

1 small **can** whole carrots (drained, rinsed & diced)

½ teaspoon vinegar

A pinch salt

A pinch sugar

1 small **can** beetroots (drained, rinsed & cut into wedges)

Method

Heat oil in a frying pan over medium flame and add curry leaves.

When the curry leaves crackle, add minced chillies and shallots and sauté till soft.

Toss in carrots, vinegar, salt and sugar and cook for a few seconds.

Toss in beetroots and cook for a few more seconds. Remove from flame.

Serve hot with bread.

Marinated Tofu & Vegetable Stir-fry (Serves 4)

A riot of colours and flavours, this quick stir-fry is a perfect side dish or main dish with any meal. Most of the preparation can be done in advance, leaving only the stir-frying to be done at the last minute.

Ingredients

FOR THE MARINADE

¼ cup **canned** vegetable broth

1 tablespoon sesame oil

2 tablespoons light soya sauce

1 tablespoon rice vinegar

½ tablespoon ginger (finely grated)

1 tablespoon lemon rind

½ tablespoon black pepper powder

200 gm firm tofu (drained & cut into large dices)

FOR THE STIR-FRY

1 tablespoon sesame oil

8 cloves garlic (minced)

2 tablespoons red chilli sauce

¼ cup peanuts (lightly roasted)

¼ cup **canned** vegetable broth

1 teaspoon sugar

1 large red capsicum (diced)

½ cup **canned** bamboo shoots (drained, rinsed well & diced)

½ cup **canned** water chestnuts in water (drained, rinsed well & cut into halves)

½ cup **canned** oyster mushrooms (drained & rinsed well)

1 small cluster bok choy (diced)

Method

In a bowl, whisk together all the ingredients required for the marinade, except tofu. Keep aside for 5 minutes, then mix in the tofu and keep aside to marinate for 10 minutes.

For the stir-fry, heat sesame oil in a wok over high flame. When the oil begins to smoke, add garlic and stir-fry for a few seconds till very fragrant.

Toss in chilli sauce, peanuts, broth and sugar, and stir quickly for a few seconds till the sugar dissolves.

Toss in all the vegetables except bok choy and stir-fry for 5 to 7 seconds.

Add tofu with the marinade and bok choy and toss very well.

Serve immediately.

Mustard Vegetable Curry
(Serves 4)

Though the most recognised form of mustard is Dijon mustard generally used as a dip, to use the same flavour in a curry is an extension of its dimensions. You can substitute vegetables with any poultry and cook it longer to create a new dish in your kitchen.

Ingredients

2 teaspoons oil

6 large cloves garlic

1 teaspoon cumin seeds

2 medium onions (finely chopped)

1 teaspoon red chilli powder

½ teaspoon turmeric powder

1 small **can** unsweetened coconut cream

1 cup **canned** vegetable broth

2 tablespoons mustard paste

1 large **can** mixed vegetables (drained & rinsed well)

Salt to taste

Method

Heat oil in a pan over medium flame. Add garlic and cumin seeds and sauté for a minute.

Add onion with chilli powder and turmeric powder and cook till the onion softens.

Stir in coconut cream with stock and bring the mixture to a boil, stirring continuously.

Allow the curry to boil for a minute, then reduce flame to low and mix in mustard paste. Simmer the curry for another 2 minutes, then add vegetables, adjust salt and remove from the flame.

Serve hot with bread or rice.

Stuffed Potato Chops with Salad (Serves 4 to 6)

This dish can impress anyone anywhere. Potato – the global favourite –combines with peas, carrots and beans to make a dish that in combination with salad makes for a great main course and on its own, is a brilliant snack.

Ingredients

FOR THE STUFFING

1 tablespoon oil

4 large cloves garlic (finely chopped)

1 medium onion (finely chopped)

1 cup **canned** peas (drained & rinsed well)

1 cup **canned** carrots (drained & rinsed well)

1 cup **canned** pinto beans (drained & rinsed well)

1 teaspoon red chilli powder

½ teaspoon turmeric powder

Salt to taste

Black pepper powder to taste

FOR THE CHOPS

8 large potatoes (boiled and peeled)

Salt to taste

Black pepper powder to taste

1 large egg (lightly beaten)

1 cup fresh breadcrumbs (plus extra for binding if required)

Oil to shallow fry

FOR THE SALAD

2 cups alfalfa sprouts

2 cups cherry tomaotes

⅓ cup golden raisins

2 tablespoons balsamic vinegar

2 tablespoons salad oil

1 teaspoon mustard paste

1 tablespoon honey

Salt to taste

Black pepper to taste (freshly ground)

⅓ cup assorted edible wild flowers

Method

For the stuffing, heat oil in a frying pan over medium flame. Add garlic and onion and sauté till the onion turns translucent.

Add peas, carrots, pinto beans, chilli powder, turmeric powder, salt and pepper and toss well to mix. Cook for a minute, mashing the mixture very lightly. Remove from flame and keep aside to cool.

Meanwhile, for the chops, rub boiled potatoes through a sieve to mash them thoroughly and mix in salt and pepper. If the mashed potato mixture seems too loose or soft, mix in 1 or 2 tablespoons breadcrumbs to aid in shaping the chops.

Divide the potato mixture and stuffing mixture into 6 equal parts. To shape, flatten a portion of the potato mixture into a disc and spoon a portion of the stuffing in the centre. Close the mashed potato around the stuffing carefully to seal it in and make a large thick patty. Repeat with the remaining stuffing and mashed potato.

To fry the chops, heat 2 tablespoons oil on a griddle. Dip the chops in egg, roll in breadcrumbs and shallow fry on the griddle on both sides (drizzling with oil if required) till golden and crisp. When done, drain on absorbent paper.

For the salad, toss all required ingredients together, except wildflowers.

Serve the stuffed potato chops hot, with salad sprinkled over with wildflowers.

Chilli Crab Mini Falafels (Serves 4 to 6)

This dish defines new-age Middle East – a mix of the traditional with the modern. The very traditional falafel is stuffed with Asian flavours resulting in a "pocket full of flavour".

Ingredients

FOR THE PITA

½ cup lukewarm water

1 teaspoon sugar

2 teaspoons dry yeast granules

1 cup milk (plus extra if required)

2 tablespoons oil

1 teaspoon salt

2 cups flour (plus extra for dusting)

FOR THE CHILLI CRAB

2 tablespoons oil

1 teaspoon ginger (minced)

5 cloves garlic (minced)

2 medium fresh red chillies (minced)

2 stalks spring onion greens (finely sliced)

1 tablespoon dark soya sauce

1 tablespoon vinegar

½ teaspoon sugar

4 tablespoons **canned** tomato passata

2 small **cans** dressed crab

Salt to taste

Black pepper powder to taste

1 medium head lettuce – any type
(torn into pieces)

MISCELLANEOUS

Cheesecloth

Method

For the pita, combine water with sugar, add yeast granules, cover and keep aside in a warm place to allow the yeast to froth.

Meanwhile whisk milk with oil and salt.

Make a well in the centre of the flour and pour yeast mixture into it. Also pour in half the milk and knead into the flour. Gradually knead in the remaining milk to make soft smooth pliable dough, dusting with more flour if required. Cover the dough with moist cheesecloth and keep in a warm place till it doubles in volume.

Preheat oven to 225°C. Grease and dust a baking tray.

When the dough doubles in volume, knead it again and divide into lemon-sized portions. Using a rolling pin, roll out each portion into an oval ½ inch thick and 4 inches long. Arrange on the baking tray and bake in the preheated oven for 2 to 5 minutes on one side. Turn the pita over and cook for another 3 to 4 minutes till the pita puffs up and turns slightly golden. Remove from the oven and cool slightly.

Cut the pita breads into half width-wise and gently open up the pockets. Keep aside.

For the chilli crab, heat oil in a wok over high flame and add ginger and garlic. Stir-fry for a minute till the ginger softens, then toss in chillies and spring onions.

Add soya sauce, vinegar, sugar and passata and stir till the sugar dissolves.

Add crab, salt and pepper and remove from flame.

To assemble, divide the lettuce into equal portions and fill into the pita pockets. Spoon the chilli crab on one side of the lettuce and serve immediately.

Grilled Aubergine Sundried Tomato & Cheese Sandwich
(Serves 4)

I generally like to grill leftover vegetables to use as a sandwich filling. However, it is worth grilling fresh vegetables especially when you are packing a picnic lunch.

Ingredients

1 large round aubergine (cut into ½-inch thick slices)

2 tablespoons oil

2 teaspoons garlic paste

2 teaspoons lemon juice

Salt to taste

Black pepper to taste (freshly ground)

2 tablespoons butter

8 slices bread

12 pieces **canned** sundried tomatoes (drained well)

1 cup cheddar cheese (finely diced)

1 small head cos lettuce

Method

Combine aubergine with oil, garlic paste, lemon juice, salt and pepper and keep aside to marinate for 15 to 20 minutes.

Heat a grill pan, brush with marinade and grill the marinated aubergine slices on both sides till tender.

To make the sandwiches, lightly butter the bread and layer the grilled aubergines, sundried tomatoes, cheese and lettuce as desired.

Serve immediately.

Hummus & Gherkin Sandwich (Serves 4 to 6)

The sourness and crunch of the gherkins are the highlights of the dish. The luscious creamy hummus makes for the perfect spread for crusty bread.

Ingredients

FOR THE HUMMUS

1 small **can** chickpeas (drained – liquid reserved – and rinsed well)

1½ tablespoons lemon juice

8 cloves garlic (roughly chopped)

½ teaspoon sea salt

1 teaspoon cumin seeds (lightly roasted)

¾ teaspoon cayenne pepper

2 medium green chillies

4 tablespoons olive oil

A few sprigs parsley (finely chopped)

FOR THE SANDWICHES

1 large loaf multigrain bread (cut into slices)

½ cup **canned** gherkins (drained well and sliced)

1 cup assorted cherry tomatoes (cut into half lengthwise)

A few sprigs parsley

Method

For the hummus, in a blender, combine chickpeas with ¼ cup reserved liquid from the can along with lemon juice, garlic, sea salt, cumin seeds, cayenne pepper and green chillies and blend till almost smooth.

Remove into a bowl and mix in olive oil and parsley.

To assemble sandwiches, simply spread hummus liberally onto bread slices, top with gherkins, cherry tomatoes and parsley and serve.

Tomato Cheese & Nut Bruschetta
(Serves 4 to 6)

I love adding a new flavour or texture to food to create a surprise element. In this case, the spiced nuts add not just their characteristic nutty flavour but also a refreshing crunch. You can also add finely chopped vegetables of your choice to up the nutrition quotient.

Ingredients

3 large tomatoes (finely diced)

½ cup cheddar cheese (finely diced)

½ cup **canned** spiced nuts (roughly chopped)

1 medium onion (finely chopped)

A few sprigs fresh basil (finely chopped)

½ tablespoon lemon juice

1 tablespoon olive oil

A pinch sugar

Salt to taste

Black pepper powder to taste

1 large loaf French bread (cut into long slices)

1 small head lettuce – any type (torn into large pieces)

Method

Combine all the ingredients except lettuce and French bread. Toss well to mix properly.

Arrange the French bread slices on a chopping board and place a piece of lettuce on each one. Spoon the tomato cheese and nut salad on each slice and serve immediately.

Tuna Salad Sandwich (Serves 4)

My first experience of going to one of the greatest fish markets in the world was in Tokyo where I saw the morning auctions of tuna. Tuna is one of the healthiest fish and the most versatile too. Because of its firm flesh, it can be used in a variety of recipes.

Ingredients

2 small **cans** tuna chunks in oil (drained well)

3 large eggs (hardboiled & diced)

10-12 pieces **canned** pitted green olives
(drained, rinsed well and roughly chopped)

½ cup mayonnaise

12 slices whole wheat bread

1 medium head lettuce – any type (torn into pieces)

2 large tomatoes (finely diced)

Method

Combine tuna chunks with eggs and olives and keep aside.

Lightly brush mayonnaise on bread slices and lay them on a chopping board.

Divide lettuce into 4 equal parts and arrange a layer of lettuce on 4 bread slices. Combine tomatoes with the remaining mayonnaise. Divide into 4 equal parts and spoon over the lettuce. Cover with the bread and press together firmly.

Divide the tuna mixture into 4 equal parts and spoon onto the prepared sandwiches. Cover with the remaining bread slices, press together firmly and serve immediately.

Herbed Orange Couscous (Serves 2)

A super-delicious, super-nutritious and super-quick dish which is very versatile too! Enjoy it for brunch, as a main course for lunch or even as a great after workout-snack!

Ingredients

2 cups **canned** unsweetened orange juice

½ teaspoon salt

1 teaspoon black pepper powder

2 inch piece ginger (finely grated)

1 teaspoon fennel seeds

2 sprigs fresh rosemary

1 cup couscous

1 small red capsicum (finely diced)

1 small green capsicum (finely diced)

6 pieces **canned** sundried tomatoes (cut into strips)

⅓ cup **canned** red lentils (drained & rinsed well)

2 teaspoons vinegar

Method

Combine orange juice with salt, pepper, ginger, fennel and rosemary in a saucepan and bring to a boil. Boil the juice for 2 minutes.

Meanwhile, combine couscous with red and green capsicum, sundried tomatoes and lentils in a big bowl.

When the juice has boiled, remove form flame Add vinegar and pour over the couscous. Stir the mixture and cover and keep aside. Fluff the mixture using a fork at regular intervals.

When the couscous has fluffed up and become tender, serve immediately.

Soup Muffins (Serves 4 to 6)

A quick warm snack perfect for chilly winter afternoons. Simply pair it with a hot cup of tea or coffee to create your own mini meal.

Ingredients

2 cups all-purpose flour

2 teaspoons baking powder

1 teaspoon soda bicarbonate

2 tablespoons parmesan cheese (grated)

1 small **can** any well-flavoured soup

½ teaspoon salt

½ teaspoon black pepper powder

¾ cup butter

3 egg yolks

MISCELLANEOUS

Muffin tray or 6 individual muffin moulds

Toothpicks

Method

Preheat oven to 180°C. Lightly grease and dust a muffin tray (or moulds).

Combine flour with baking powder and soda bicarbonate and sift thrice. Mix in cheese.

Mix soup with salt and pepper and keep aside.

Cream butter with egg yolks using a wooden spoon. Gradually fold in the flour and soup alternately to make a thick batter.

Pour into the muffin tray (or moulds) and bake for 15 to 18 minutes or till the toothpick inserted in the centre comes clean.

Serve hot or cool.

Chocolate Raspberry Fudge
(Serves 4)

The dense chocolate combined with raspberries is a perfect dessert and a great gourmet gift! I generally prefer dark chocolate for a greater echo of flavours.

Ingredients

½ cup unsalted butter

½ cup dark cooking chocolate (roughly chopped)

1 **can** sweetened condensed milk

⅓ cup sugar

¼ cup Dutch cocoa powder

¼ teaspoon angostura bitters

1 cup **canned** raspberry pie filling

MISCELLANEOUS

Small well-greased baking tray

Method

In a large heavy pan, combine butter, chocolate, condensed milk, sugar and cocoa and cook over medium flame, stirring continuously with a wooden spoon till the chocolate melts and all the ingredients mix thoroughly.

Continue cooking till the mixture begins to thicken. Add angostura bitters and raspberry pie filling and continue cooking till the mixture begins to leave the sides of the pan. (In case you feel the fudge is burning, reduce the flame and remove the pan from the flame at regular intervals.)

When the mixture starts leaving the sides of the pan, pour into the prepared baking tray and smoothen the surface. Keep aside to cool to room temperature.

When the mixture is just lukewarm, score out pieces using a well-greased knife. When the fudge cools completely, cut out pieces and serve.

Phirni Custard with Mixed Fruits

(Serves 4 to 6)

The earthy taste of basmati rice is unmatched with any other variety of rice. I feel very happy to see this variety of rice readily available in supermarkets around the world. The beautiful strands of saffron floating and colouring this decadent dessert will definitely win you tons of compliments.

Ingredients

1 cup basmati or long-grain rice (washed, soaked for 10 minutes & drained)

3½ cups whole milk

1 cup **canned** sweetened condensed milk

1 teaspoon saffron strands (dissolved in 3 tablespoons warm milk)

½ teaspoon cardamom powder

¼ cup sugar (optional)

1 small **can** mixed fruits in syrup (drained well)

Method

Combine rice with ¾ cup milk in a grinder and grind to a coarse paste.

Bring the remaining milk to a boil over medium high flame, add rice paste, reduce flame to low and cook, stirring continuously till the rice is cooked. Stir in condensed milk, saffron (with milk) and cardamom powder (and sugar – if using) and as soon as the mixture thickens, remove from flame.

Divide the phirni custard equally into 6 bowls, top with mixed fruit and serve.

Alternately, refrigerate the phirni custard and fruits separately and serve chilled.

Pineapple Mandarin Upside-Down Cake (Serves 6 to 8)

This is my favourite cake when I teach bakery. The placement of fruits is great for beginners who find "icing a cake" a daunting task. Make sure you cool the cake in the tin for a couple of minutes once it's out of the oven – this will ensure it holds well.

Ingredients

FOR THE FRUIT LINING

1 tablespoon butter

3 tablespoons sugar

1 small **can** pineapple rings in syrup (drained well)

1 small **can** mandarin segments in syrup (drained well)

FOR THE CAKE

1 cup all-purpose flour

1 teaspoon baking powder

½ teaspoon soda bicarbonate

½ cup butter

½ **can** sweetened condensed milk

¾ cup milk

A few drops vanilla essence

MISCELLANEOUS

Small cake tin

Toothpicks

Cooling rack

Method

Melt butter in cake tin and swirl tin around to coat base and sides evenly with butter. Add sugar, place the tin over medium flame and allow the sugar to caramelise to a rich golden brown. Swirl the cake tin slightly to coat base evenly with caramel.

Quickly and carefully place the pineapple rings and mandarin segments on the caramel-covered base in any design you like. Keep the tin aside.

Preheat oven to 165°C.

Combine flour with baking powder and soda bicarbonate and sift the mixture thrice.

In a large mixing bowl, combine butter with condensed milk and whisk till light and frothy.

Fold in the flour alternately with milk to make a thick batter. Mix in vanilla essence and pour the batter in the prepared cake tin.

Bake in the preheated oven for 18 to 20 minutes or till the cake is golden on top and the toothpick inserted in the centre comes clean.

When done, remove from the oven and wait 2 minutes before inverting the cake onto a cooling rack. Cool completely before cutting.

Roast Peaches with Coconut Walnut Sauce (Serves 4)

Once I was asked what my favourite food was. I replied, "A perfectly ripe sweet peach." It is an essential part of a Chef's life to fall in love with dense sweet peaches. Feel free to substitute peaches with plums or apples or pears if peaches aren't your favourite.

Ingredients

FOR THE SAUCE

1 tablespoon butter

3 tablespoons walnut powder

1 cup **canned** sweetened coconut cream

FOR THE PEACHES

2 teaspoons butter

2 tablespoons sugar

1 large **can** peach slices in syrup (drained well)

FOR GARNISH

3 tablespoons walnuts (crushed)

A few sprigs fresh mint

Method

For the sauce, heat butter in a frying pan over low flame. When the butter melts, add walnut powder and cook, stirring continuously till the walnuts smell lightly roasted.

Gradually stir in coconut cream and cook, stirring continuously till the sauce simmers. Remove from flame and keep aside.

For the peaches, heat butter in a frying pan over medium flame. Add sugar and cook till the sugar is caramelised to rich golden brown. Add peaches and toss well to coat. Roast in the pan for a minute.

To serve, divide the sauce equally over 4 dessert plates and spoon peaches over it. Sprinkle with walnuts and mint and serve immediately.

Warm Pear Crumble (Serves 4)

Called crumble in USA and crisp in UK, whatever the name, the result is always a warm crunch complementing soft mellow fruit. The natural sugar in the fruits caramelise while baking, giving them a dense flavour which combines very well with the crunchy crust.

Ingredients

FOR THE CRUMBLE

1 cup all-purpose flour (plus extra for dusting)

½ cup butter (chilled & cut into cubes)

1 egg (lightly beaten)

FOR THE PEARS

1 tablespoon butter

⅓ cup sugar

⅓ cup cream

¼ teaspoon cinnamon powder

¼ cup **canned** unsweetened white grape juice

8 pieces **canned** pear halves in syrup (drained well)

FOR GARNISH

A few sprigs fresh mint

MISCELLANEOUS

Lightly greased baking tray

Method

For the crumble, using your fingertips, crumble the flour and butter together till the mixture resembles breadcrumbs.

Lightly but quickly knead in the egg to make smooth semi-firm dough. Wrap the dough in clingfilm and refrigerate for 30 minutes.

Meanwhile, for the pears, melt butter in a heavy pan over medium flame and add sugar. Caramelise the sugar till it is rich golden brown. Remove from flame and whisk in cream, cinnamon and grape juice.

Cook the cream caramel till it comes to a simmer. Toss in the pear halves curved side down and cook for a minute. Remove from flame and keep warm.

Preheat oven to 165°C. Remove the pastry dough from the refrigerator and rub through a sieve with large holes to make even crumbs. Spread the crumbs evenly over the baking tray and bake in the preheated oven for 7 to 8 minutes till the crumble is just baked crisp and light golden.

To serve, arrange 2 pear halves in each of 4 dessert plates with a spoonful of sauce. Sprinkle over liberally with the prepared crumbs. Garnish with mint and serve warm.

Breakfast Juice
(Serves 4)

Breakfast – the most important meal of the day – just got easier and quicker. This quick breakfast drink gives you enough energy to start your day and is delicious.

Ingredients

1 large **can** tomato juice

1 large **can** sliced carrots (drained & rinsed well)

1 small **can** beetroots (drained & rinsed well)

15-18 leaves fresh mint

2 sprigs celery

4 cloves garlic (roughly chopped)

3 cups water or ice

Salt to taste

Black pepper powder to taste

Method

Combine all the ingredients except salt and pepper in a blender and blend till smooth. Strain into a jug and mix in salt and pepper.

Serve immediately.

Carrot Pear Ginger Juice (Serves 2 to 3)

This juice is not only healthy but delicious enough to replace dessert. Great for those who believe in eating light, thus making it a great substitute for desserts, add vanilla ice cream if you wish to.

Ingredients

1 small **can** sliced carrots (drained & rinsed well)

1 small **can** pears in syrup (drained well)

1 teaspoon ginger juice

2 tablespoons honey

2 cups ice

Method

Combine all the ingredients in a blender and blend till smooth. Strain and serve immediately.

Mixed Berry Smoothie (Serves 4 to 6)

A filling beverage that you can enjoy for breakfast, lunch or a quick evening meal. Simply replace the berries or add more fruits for a greater range of flavours.

Ingredients

4 cups plain yoghurt

1 small **can** raspberries in syrup (drained well)

1 small **can** blueberries in syrup (drained well)

2 tablespoons honey (or more as per taste)

1 teaspoon lemon rind

2 cups ice

Method

Combine all the ingredients in a blender and blend till smooth and frothy. Serve immediately.

Orange Lychee Pineapple Juice
(Serves 4)

The tropical sweetness of oranges, lychees and pineapples is balanced interestingly with pepper and lemon. Cinnamon lends it just the right touch of warmth to give it a hint of the festive taste.

Ingredients

750 ml fresh orange juice

1 large **can** pineapple juice

1 small **can** lychees in syrup (drained well)

¼ teaspoon white pepper powder

1 tablespoon lemon juice

1 tablespoon cinnamon powder

½ tablespoon sugar

Method

Combine orange juice and pineapple juice with lychees in a mixer or blender and blend till smooth. Strain into a jug and mix in pepper. Refrigerate to chill.

To serve, brush the rims of 4 glasses with lemon juice and rim with cinnamon powder and sugar. Pour in the juice and serve chilled.

Peach Strawberry Sparkle (Serves 6)

A great drink to serve at parties. It's a much healthier alternative to artificially sweetened carbonated drinks. You can also substitute the soda with fresh chilled water.

Ingredients

1 large **can** peach slices in syrup (drained well)

2 cups fresh strawberries (roughly chopped)

12 cubes ice

6 **cans** ginger ale or plain soda

Method

Combine peaches and strawberries in a blender and blend till smooth. Divide the juice equally into 6 glasses and add 2 cubes of ice in each glass.

Top each glass up with a can of ginger ale or soda and serve immediately.

Pepper Hot
Chocolate (Serves 5)

Cold and tired but can't fall asleep? This is a sure-shot remedy. The creamy luscious hot chocolate fills you with cosy warmth while pepper adds a fragrant touch of flavour.

Ingredients

3 tablespoons **canned** Dutch cocoa

3 tablespoons **canned** milk powder

5 cups water

2 tablespoons sugar

¼ cup heavy cream

½ teaspoon mixed pepper (freshly ground)

Method

Whisk cocoa and milk powder into water till well mixed and bring to a boil.

Boil for 2 to 3 minutes, then add sugar and boil till the sugar dissolves.

Reduce flame and mix in cream and freshly ground pepper. Simmer for 2 minutes, then serve hot.

Kitchen Measurement Conversion Tables

Liquid or Volume Measures (approximate)

1 teaspoon		⅓ tablespoon	5 ml	
1 tablespoon	½ fluid ounce	3 teaspoons	15 ml	15 cc
2 tablespoons	1 fluid ounce	⅛ cup, 6 teaspoons	30 ml,	30 cc
¼ cup	2 fluid ounces	4 tablespoons	59 ml	
⅓ cup	2⅔ fluid ounces	5 tablespoons & 1 teaspoon	79 ml	
½ cup	4 fluid ounces	8 tablespoons	118 ml	
⅓ cup	5⅓ fluid ounces	10 tablespoons & 2 teaspoons	158 ml	
¾ cup	6 fluid ounces	12 tablespoons	177 ml	
⅞ cup	7 fluid ounces	14 tablespoons	207 ml	
1 cup	8 fluid ounces/ ½ pint	16 tablespoons	237 ml	
2 cups	16 fluid ounces/ 1 pint	32 tablespoons	473 ml	
4 cups	32 fluid ounces	1 quart	946 ml	
1 pint	16 fluid ounces/ 1 pint	32 tablespoons	473 ml	
2 pints	32 fluid ounces	1 quart	946 ml	0.946 litres
8 pints	1 gallon/ 128 fluid ounces	4 quarts	3785 ml	3.78 litres
4 quarts	1 gallon/128 fluid ounces	1 gallon	3785 ml	3.78 litres
1 litre	1.057 quarts		1000 ml	
1 gallon	4 quarts	128 fluid ounces	3785 ml	3.78 litres

Dry or Weight Measurements (approximate)

1 ounce		30 grammes (28.35 g)
2 ounces		55 grammes
3 ounces		85 grammes
4 ounces	¼ pound	125 grammes
8 ounces	½ pound	240 grammes
12 ounces	¾ pound	375 grammes
16 ounces	1 pound	454 grammes
32 ounces	2 pounds	907 grammes
¼ pound	4 ounces	125 grammes
½ pound	8 ounces	240 grammes
¾ pound	12 ounces	375 grammes
1 pound	16 ounces	454 grammes
2 pounds	32 ounces	907 grammes
1 kilogramme	2.2 pounds/ 35.2 ounces	1000 grammes

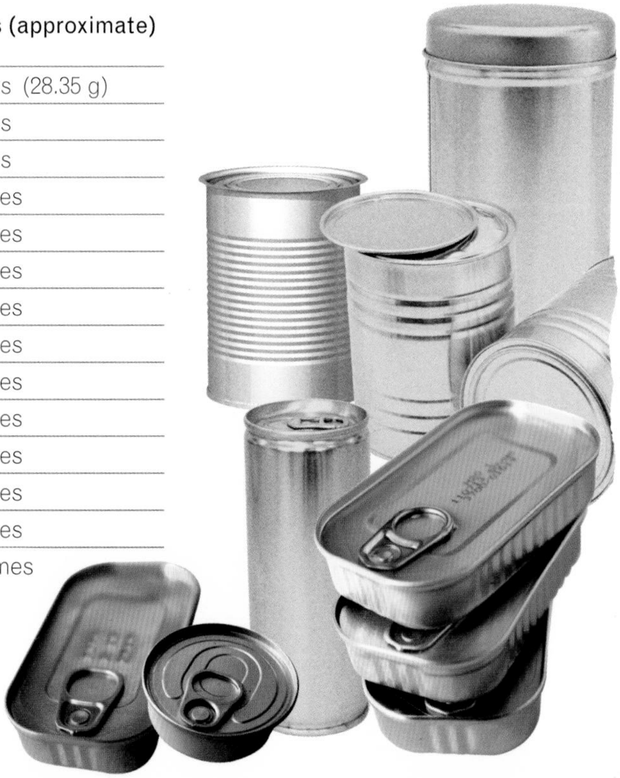

Conversions
Fahrenheit to Centigrade: Subtract 32, multiply by 5, divide by 9.
Centigrade to Fahrenheit: Multiply by 9, divide by 5, add 32.